5-8

LOST BOY

THE STORY OF THE MAN WHO CREATED

Peter Pan

"*I ought to mention here that the following is our way with a story. First I tell it to him, and then he tells it to me, the understanding being that it is quite a different story; and then I retell it with his additions, and so we go on until no one could say whether it is more his story or mine.*"

FROM PETER PAN IN KENSINGTON GARDENS

LOST BOY

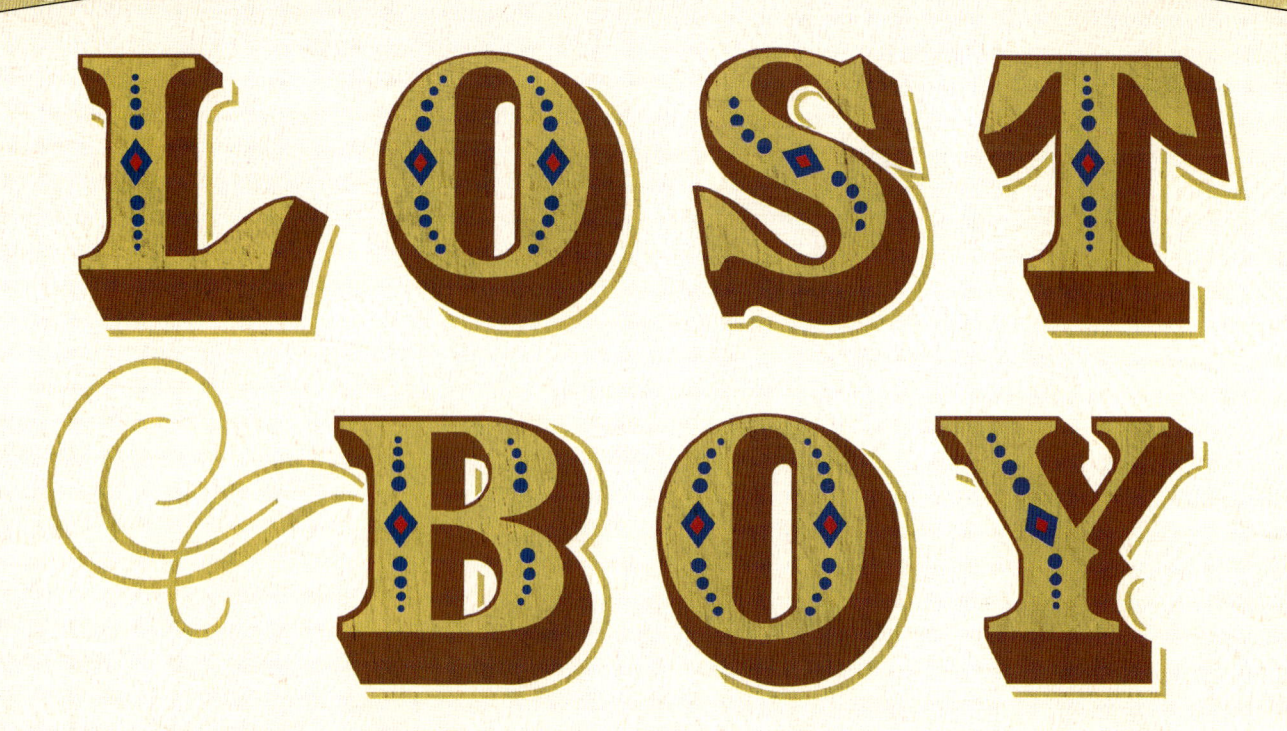

THE STORY OF THE MAN WHO CREATED

Peter Pan

BY JANE YOLEN

ILLUSTRATED BY STEVE ADAMS

◆ Dutton Children's Books ◆

An imprint of Penguin Group (USA) Inc.

"All of ‹the birds› were asleep, including the sentinels, except Solomon, who was wide awake on one side, and he listened quietly to Peter's adventures, and then told him their true meaning."

FROM PETER PAN IN KENSINGTON GARDENS

*To the memory of David Stemple, my life's companion,
though his life was shorter than mine*
—J.Y.

To my sister, Lynn
—S.A.

Text copyright © 2010 by Jane Yolen
Illustrations copyright © 2010 by Steve Adams
All rights reserved.

Library of Congress Cataloging-in-Publication Data
Yolen, Jane.
Lost boy : the story of the man who created Peter Pan / by Jane Yolen ; illustrated by Steve Adams.—1st ed.   p. cm.
Includes bibliographical references.
ISBN 978-0-525-47886-7 (hardcover)
1. Barrie, J. M. (James Matthew), 1860–1937—Juvenile literature.
2. Authors, Scottish—20th century—Biography—Juvenile literature.
3. Barrie, J. M. (James Matthew), 1860–1937. Peter Pan—Juvenile literature. I. Adams, Steve, 1967– ill. II. Title.
PR4076.Y65 2010   828'.91209—dc22   [B]   2009024697

Published in the United States by Dutton Children's Books,
a division of Penguin Young Readers Group
345 Hudson Street, New York, New York 10014
www.penguin.com/youngreaders

Designed by Heather Wood
Manufactured in China | First Edition
1 3 5 7 9 10 8 6 4 2

AUTHOR'S NOTE | A few of the many books I consulted are:
Barrie, J. M., *A Window in Thrums*. Chicago: Donohue & Henneberry & Co.
Barrie, J. M., *The Little White Bird or Adventures in Kensington Gardens*. New York: Charles Scribner's & Sons, 1902.
Barrie, J. M., *M'Connachie and J.M.B: Speeches by J. M. Barrie*. New York: Charles Scribner's Sons, 1939.
Barrie, J. M., *Peter Pan and Other Plays*. Oxford: Oxford University Press, 1995.
Barrie, J. M., *Peter and Wendy*. Oxford: Oxford University Press, 1999.
Barrie, J. M., *Peter Pan in Kensington Gardens*. New York: Charles Scribner's & Sons, 1913.
Barrie, J. M., *Tommy and Grizel*. New York: Charles Scribner's & Sons, 1912.
Birkin, Andrew, *J.M. Barrie and the Lost Boys*. New Haven: Yale University Press, 2003.
Darlington, W. A., *J. M. Barrie*. New York: Haskell House Publishers, Ltd., 1974.
Ormond, Leonee, *J. M. Barrie*. Scottish Writers Series, Edinburgh, Scottish Academic Press, 1987.
Walbrook, H. M., *J. M. Barrie and the Theatre*. Honolulu, University Press of the Pacific, 1969, 2003.
Wullschlager, Jackie, *Inventing Wonderland*. New York: The Free Press, 1995.
Young, Timothy G, *My Heart in Company: The Work of J. M. Barrie and the Birth of Peter Pan*. New Haven, Connecticut: Yale University, 2005.

*"He was not so much a great artist
—though the sanest critic knew he was that, too—
as a man who could see visions."*

FROM THE DAILY TELEGRAPH ON BARRIE'S DEATH IN 1937

*"I am a capable artist;
but it begins to look to me as if you are a man of genius."*

R. L. STEVENSON IN A LETTER TO BARRIE

"You are the best man among us."

FROM THE ADMIRAL CRICHTON, THE PLAY

O NCE UPON A TIME, on May 9, 1860, a baby boy was born in a low-built house, one of a row of such houses known as The Tenements, in the small town of Kirriemuir in Scotland. He was the seventh child, third boy.

James Matthew Barrie wrote that his birth was of such little event in the family, what was celebrated on that day was that they'd bought six chairs. He talked of their poverty and how little they had. But though it was a story that he elaborated on for the rest of his life, it was not strictly true.

"One girl is worth more than twenty boys."
FROM PETER PAN, THE PLAY

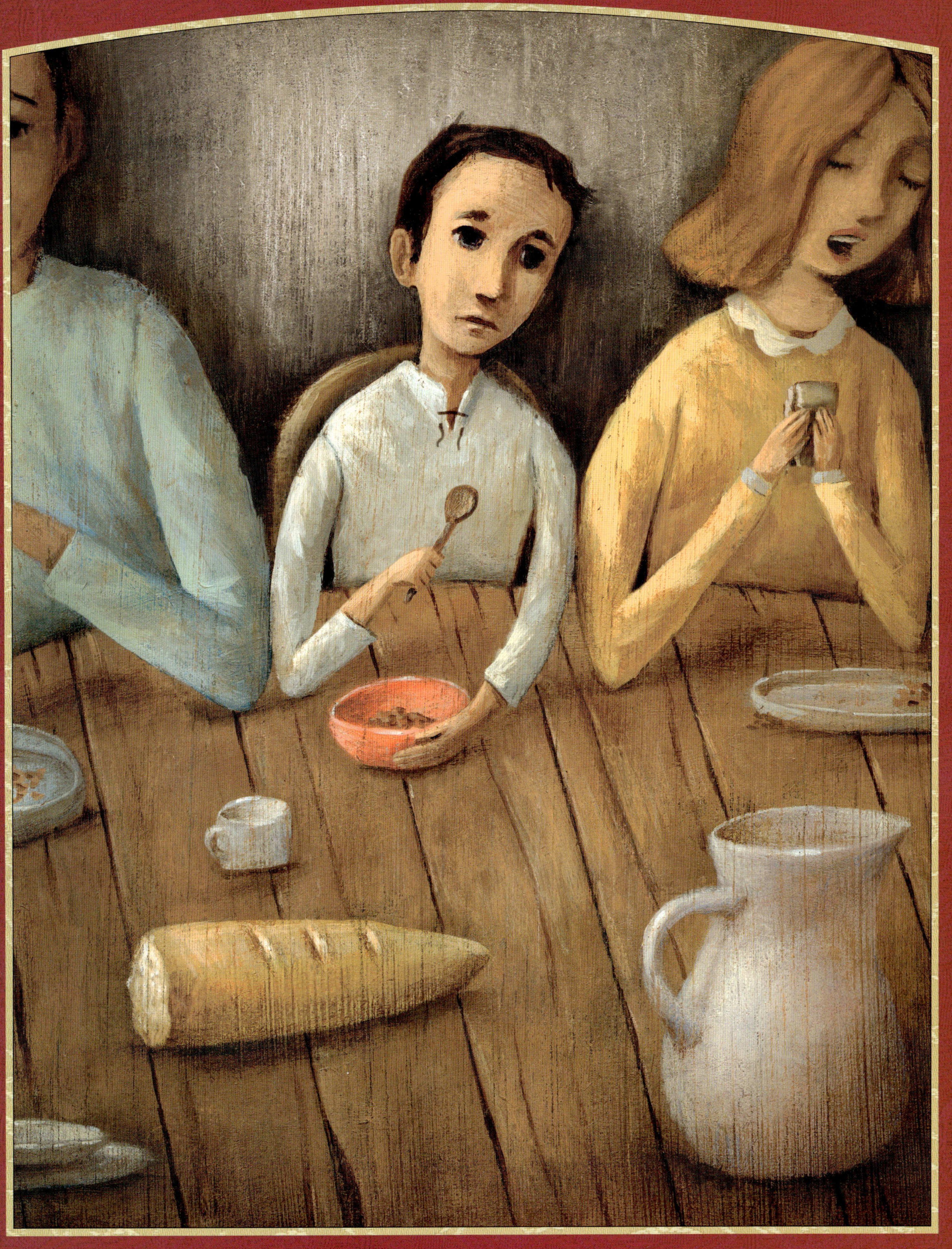

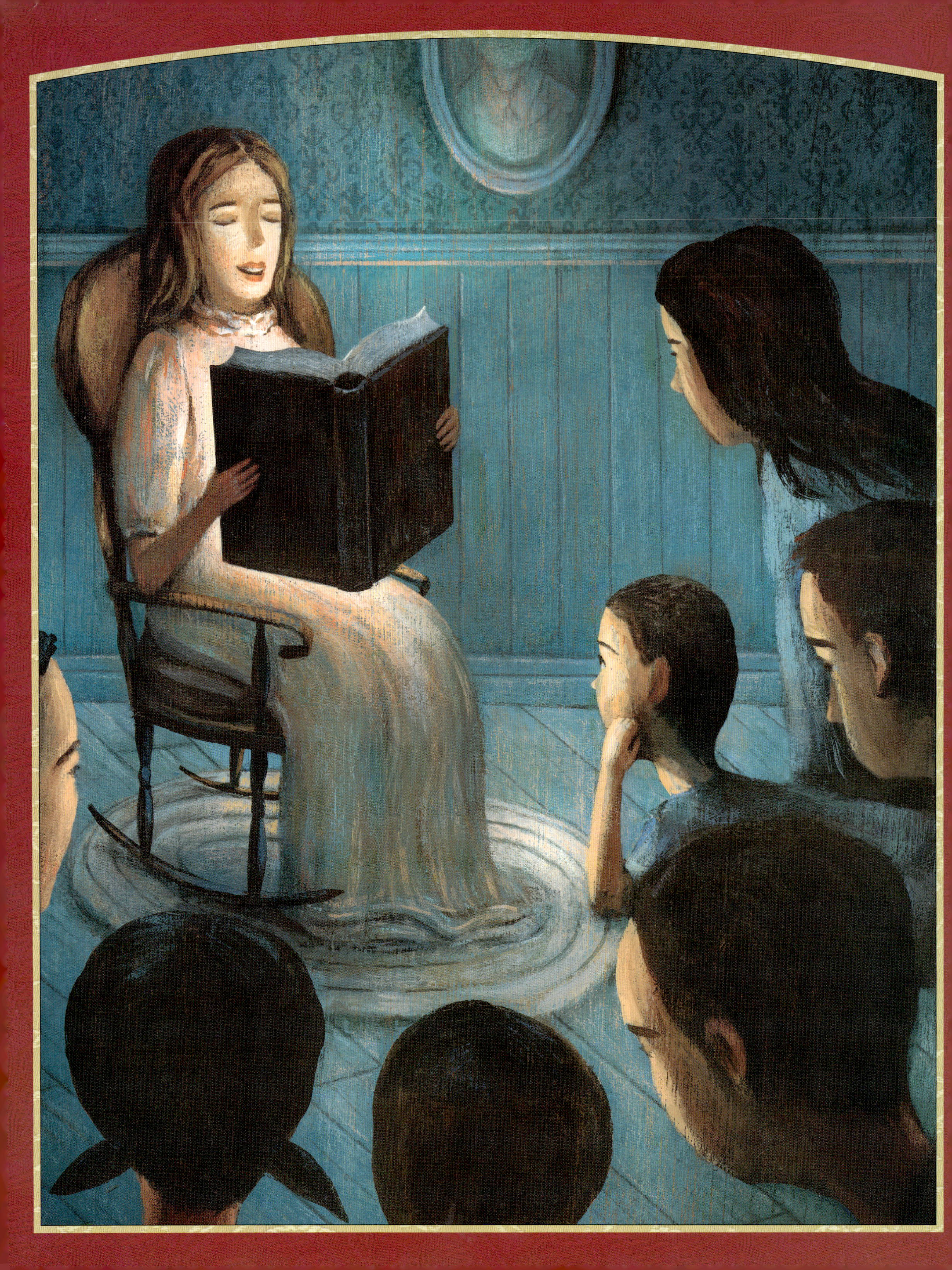

Actually, Mr. Barrie was a moderately prosperous hand-loom weaver. And while the large family was crowded into their small tenement house, they were not so different from their neighbors.

Most of the family's daily living was done in the two rooms upstairs. Mr. Barrie's loom took up one of the small rooms in the downstairs, while another small room held the prepared cloth. The children—four girls and three boys—slept in box beds in the cloth room.

In the evenings, mother Margaret sat by the hearth and the children gathered around her. There she told stories about her own growing up, and read to them books like *Robinson Crusoe,* which they got from the library for a penny a day.

*"(S)he was just slightly disappointed
when he admitted that he came to the nursery window
not to see her but to listen to stories."*

FROM PETER AND WENDY

Even as a child, Jamie was a storyteller, a gift he inherited from his mother. Whenever his favorite magazine, *Sunshine*, didn't arrive on time, he would write stories himself. Up in the top floor of the house, he scribbled away.

Then he'd run down the stairs with one story after another which he read to his mother as she sat making rag rugs.

"He was a poet;
and they are never exactly grown-up."

FROM PETER PAN IN KENSIBBLED GARDENS

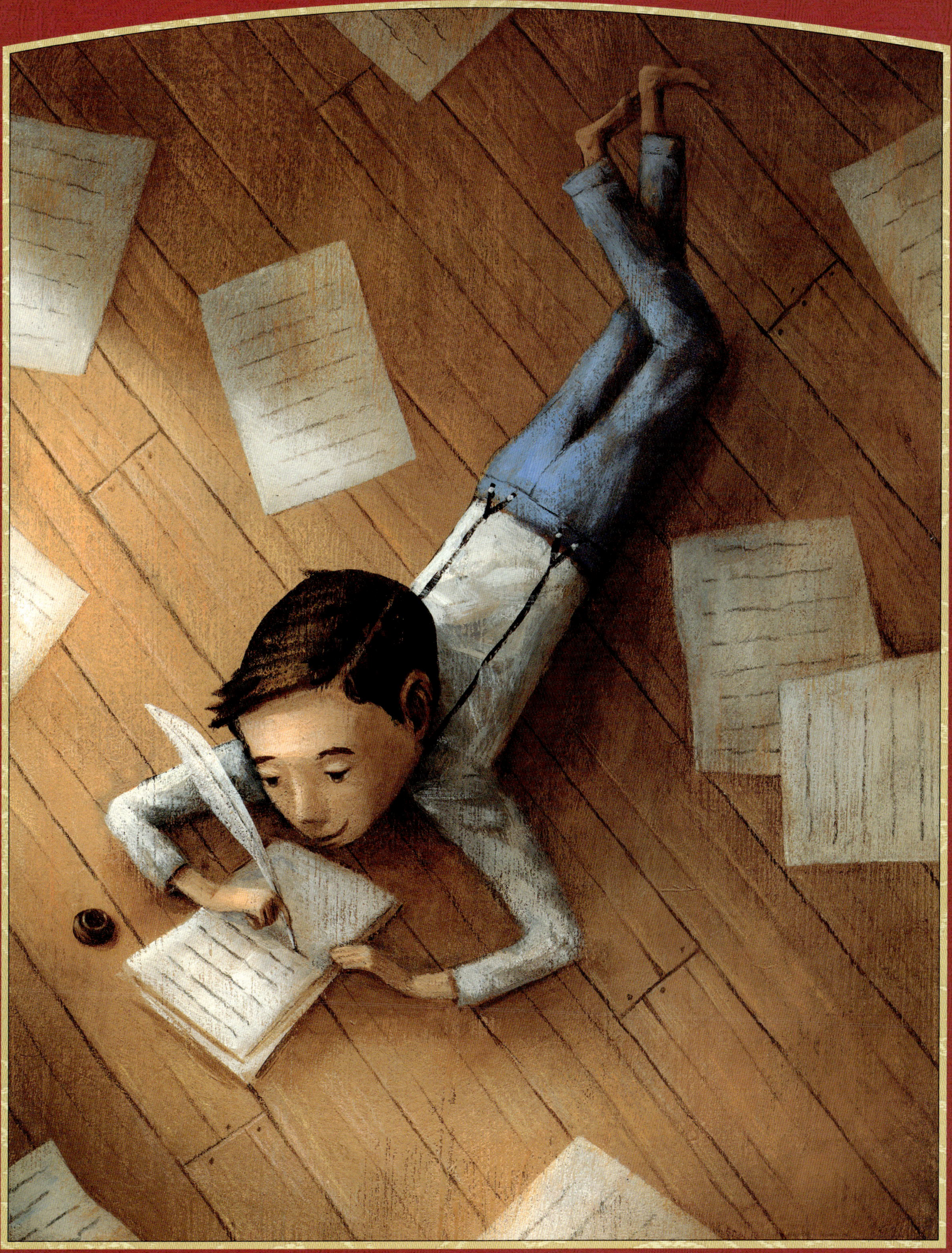

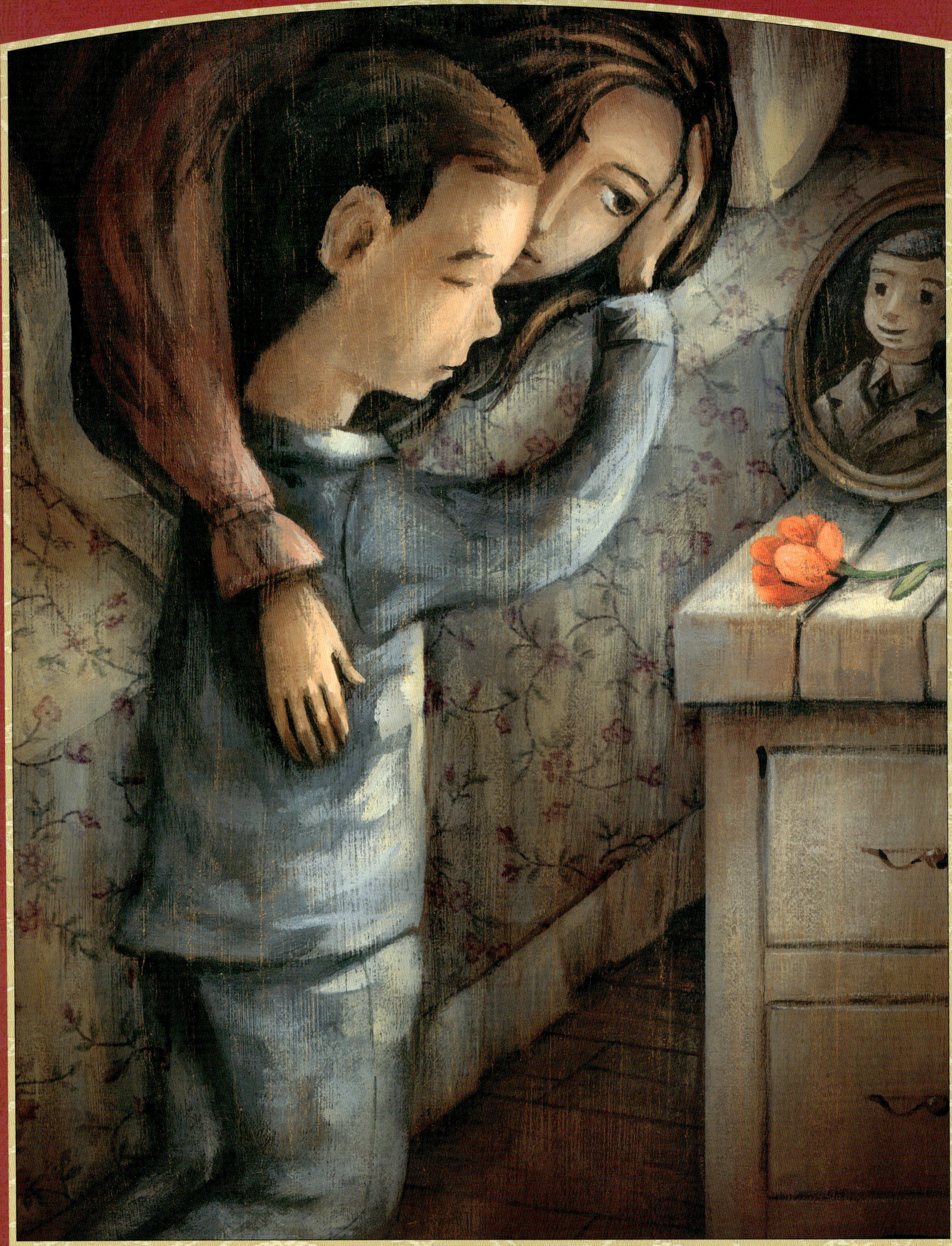

When Jamie was six, his oldest brother, Alexander, had already graduated from Aberdeen University and opened his own private school.

His next oldest brother, David, was thirteen, the family's golden boy. Tall and handsome, he was good at athletics. Then in January of 1867, on the eve of his fourteenth birthday, the golden David fell on the ice and died.

Mrs. Barrie took to her bed in a darkened room and would not come out for many days, weeping loudly.

Weeks later, seeing young Jamie sobbing on the stairs, one of his sisters urged him to go into the darkened room and speak to their mother, to remind her that she still had another young son.

In went Jamie. The door shut behind him. And then he heard his mother call out, "Is that you?" Then again: "Is that you?"

Without thinking, he replied in a little, lonely voice, "No, it's not him, it's just me."

He heard his mother weep, turn in the bed, and hold out her arms to him. Jamie rushed into her embrace.

"Boy, why are you crying?"

WENDY TO PETER, FROM PETER AND WENDY

The family mourned for many months, but eventually Jamie found his own spirit again. Outside the Kirriemuir tenement, in his mother's washhouse, he began putting on plays he wrote with his friend Robb, many of which were based on Bible stories. The boys charged the other children "preens, a boul, or a peerie" to watch the plays. That is: "pins, a marble, or a top."

The plays usually ended with the two boys trying to tip one another into the washtub, to the delight and cheering of all.

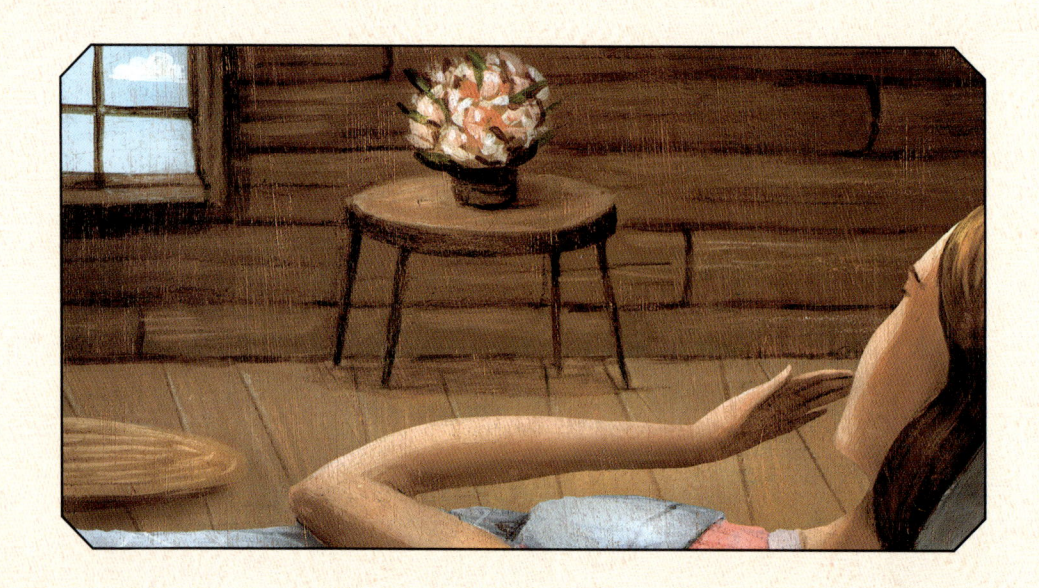

"Lovely, darling house."

FROM PETER PAN, THE PLAY

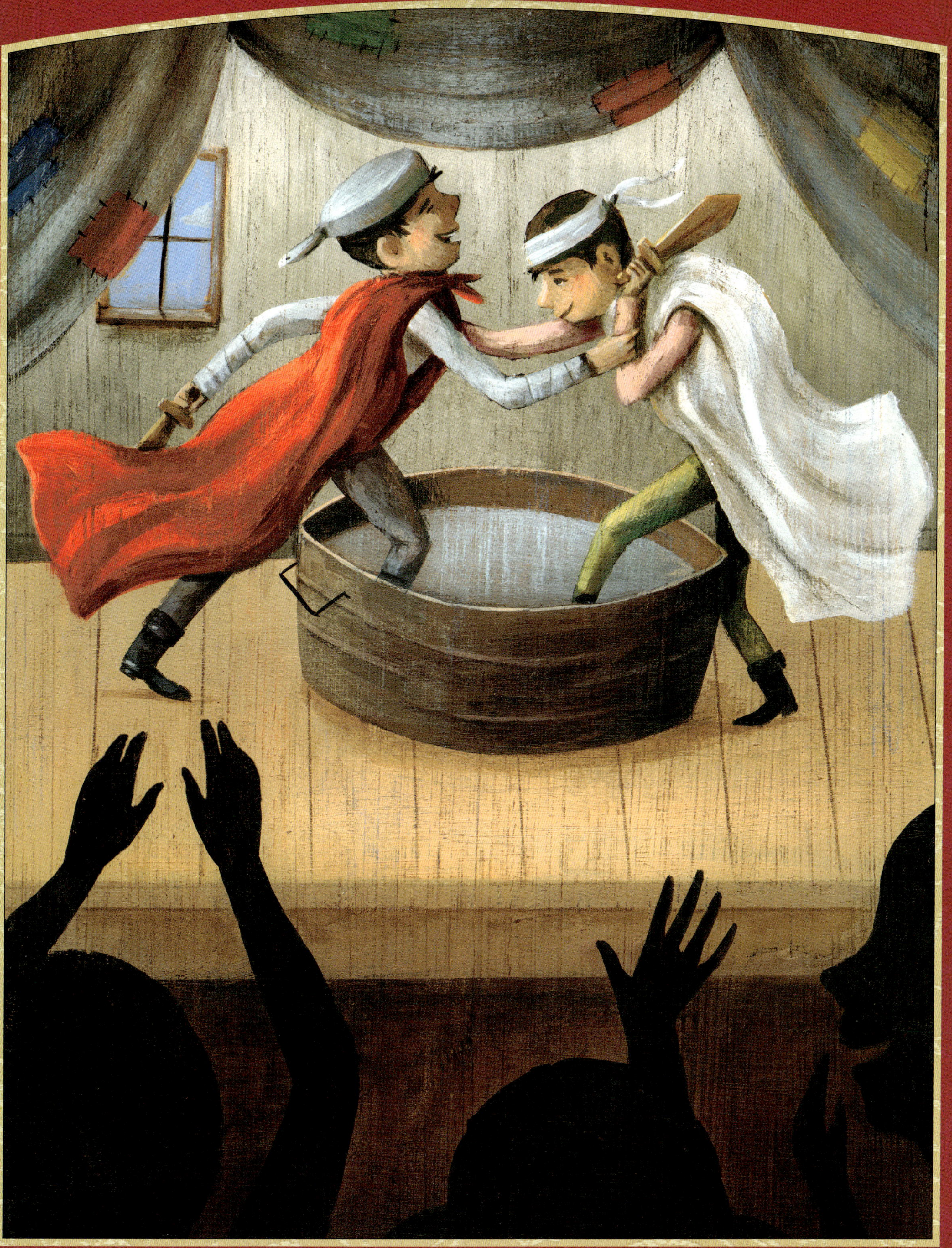

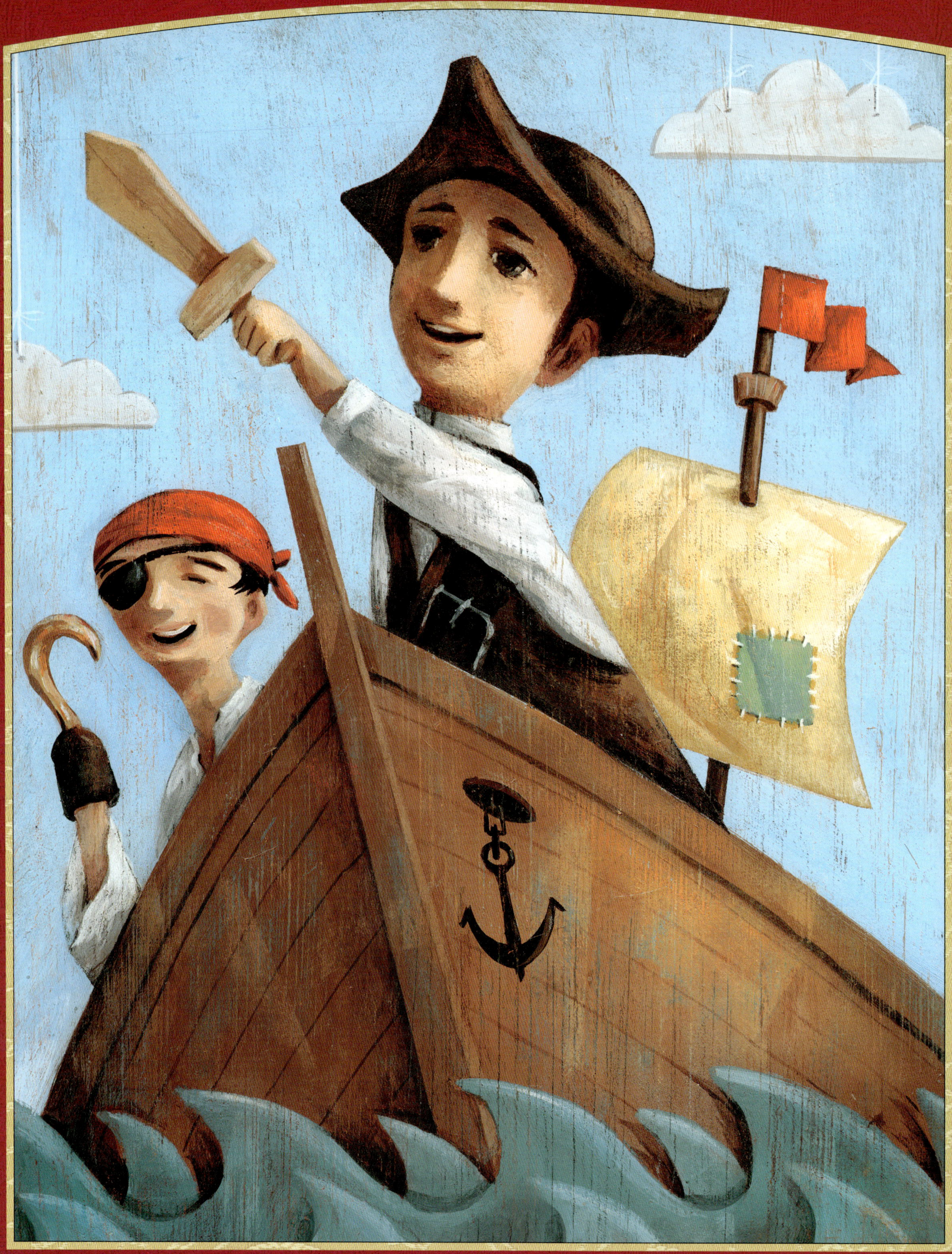

When he turned eight, Jamie was sent off to Glasgow to live with his older brother, Alick. He was homesick for his sisters and didn't enjoy the school at all. So when his father changed jobs and was working in Forfar, Jamie came back to the family to go to school there.

He was no happier.

His father got an even better job, and they moved back to Kirriemuir where Jamie spent a year at Kirriemuir Academy. Finally he was sent off to Dumfries with his brother, Alick, now an Inspector of Schools for the area. Between 1873–1878, Jamie stayed at Dumfries Academy.

At last he was happy in school. He joined the Debating Society. He went on fishing expeditions. And he met a boy named Stuart Gordon who shared his interest in stories and "penny dreadfuls," which were cheap, eight-page adventure books.

Jamie and Stuart took to calling one another "Sixteen String Jack" for Jamie, and "Dare Devil Dick" for Stuart, after characters in the books. Dare Devil Dick was a boy who ran off to sea to join a pirate ship. The boys played at being pirates together. Barrie even kept a book of their escapades, a kind of logbook. He was later to write that those five years were the happiest of his life.

"Oh why can't you remain like this forever?"

FROM PETER AND WENDY

It was in Dumfries that Jamie Barrie went to a real theater for the first time. He was so taken by his experience, he began a theatrical society at school with a handful of other boys. In their first season, he wrote a play for the society—*Bandelero the Bandit*. It was a "penny dreadful" kind of play.

A local clergyman denounced it in the newspaper, calling it gross and immoral. Jamie was delighted by the attack and wrote to a number of famous theater people enlisting their support. The London papers wrote about the play and its author. Jamie had his first taste of celebrity.

*"How clever I am,"
he crowed rapturously,
"oh, the cleverness of me!"*

FROM **PETER AND WENDY**

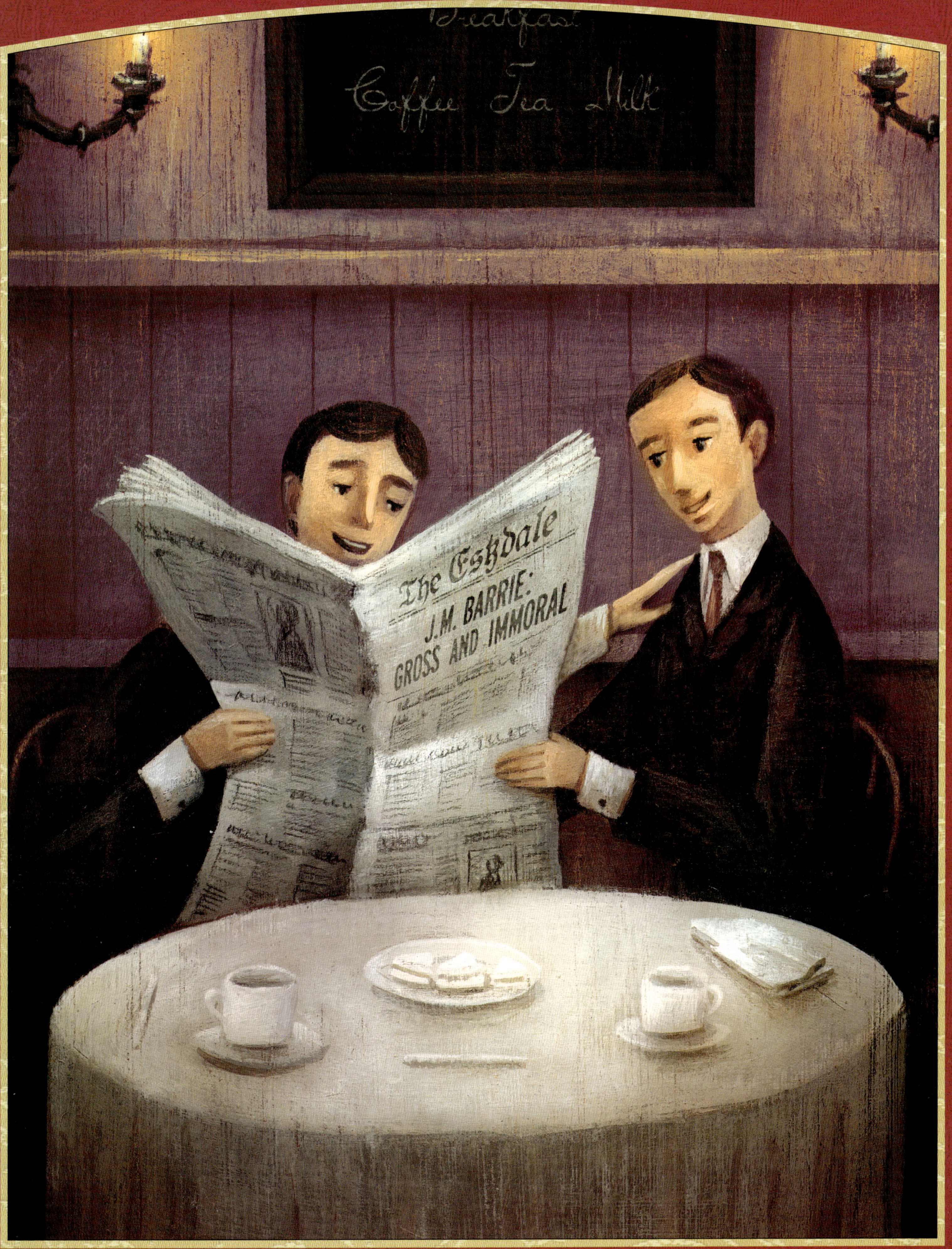
Coffee Tea Milk
The Eskdale
J.M. BARRIE:
GROSS AND IMMORAL

CARTES OPERA COMPANY
H.M.S. PINAFORE
OPERA COMIQUE
H.M.S PINAFORE
THE CHILDREN'S PINAFORE
THE CHILDREN'S PINAFORE

After graduation, Jamie returned home, determined to be a writer.

He filled a series of notebooks with his ideas. But his parents insisted that he go off to Edinburgh University.

He was not a good student.

Still, he did accomplish something. He fell in love with the theater all over again, for Edinburgh was a city of theaters. He wrote reviews of plays he'd seen. Book reviews, too. And after graduating in 1882, he began writing in earnest, sending off a series of articles to London magazines. To be published in London was what all *real* writers longed for.

In his own estimation he was pencil-thin, inarticulate in company, and with "manners, full of nails like his boots." Nobody but he thought he would make his way in the world.

"Peter, Peter, you are wasting the faerie dust."

FROM THE PLAYLET, "WENDY, AN AFTERTHOUGHT"

By 1884, the *St. James Gazette* in London had published a number of Jamie's stories about a make-believe Scottish town called Thrums, which were based on his mother's memories and the stories she used to tell the children. "Thrums" are waste threads that hang from a skein winder, something Jamie would have known about from the days when his father had been a hand weaver.

When Jamie sent the editor of the *Gazette* a new story about Thrums, called "The Rooks Begin to Build," he heard nothing for days. Nervous but determined, he packed his square wooden university box and took the all-night train to London.

When he arrived in London, he saw a placard on a newsstand announcing the latest copy of the *Gazette*. His story about the Rooks was listed prominently among the pieces.

What a good sign that was!

"I'm youth, I'm joy,
I'm a little bird that has broken out of the egg."

PETER TO HOOK, FROM PETER PAN, THE PLAY

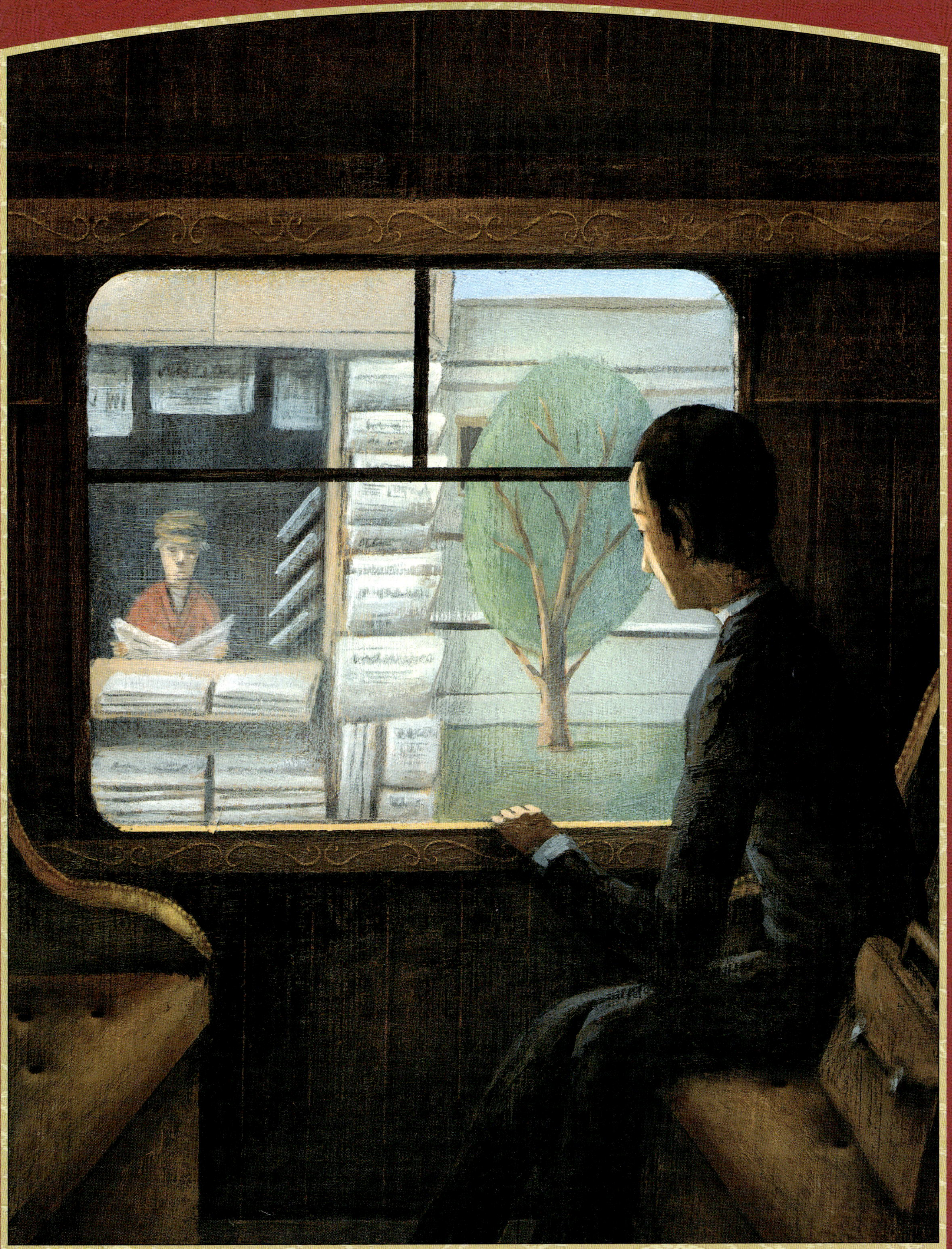

J. M. BARRIE
THE LITTLE MINISTER
J. M. BARRIE
J. M. BARRIE
J. M. BARRIE
J. M. BARRIE

Within three years, his writing had been published in all the best magazines in Britain. "Hard work," he wrote, "more than any woman in the world, is the one who stands up best for her man."

He felt ready to write a novel, but could get no one to publish it, so he brought it out himself, losing twenty-five pounds in the process, a considerable sum of money in those days.

For his next project, he gathered up all his stories about Thrums. It and its sequel made Jamie a reputation as a popular writer.

But it was his next book, a novel about Thrums called *The Little Minister*, that gained him a worldwide reputation. In fact, at the Kirriemuir post office one could now buy picture postcards with pictures of the make-believe Thrums on it.

Jamie was a famous man. However, he was still as small as a boy, just over five feet tall, thin, with a reedy high-pitched voice. He hardly looked famous.

*"It's a pity I'm so little, Mother,"
he said with a sigh.*

FROM THE LITTLE MINISTER

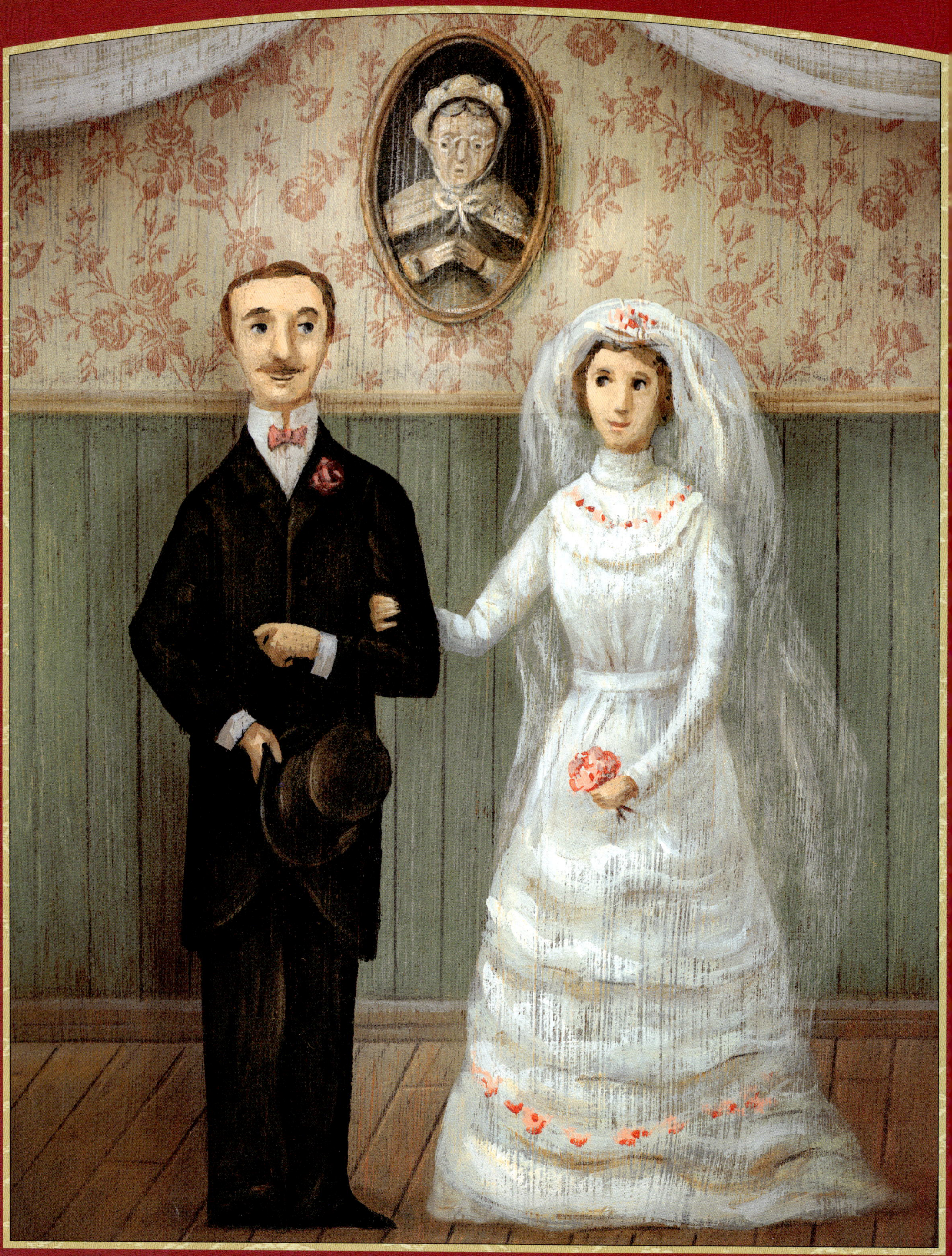

Though his success was with magazine articles and books, Barrie's first love was still the theater. In 1891 he wrote the play *Richard Savage* with a friend. It had only one performance. Two months later he tried his hand at parody—*Isben's Ghost*. That at least was a success, though a small one.

A year later his next play, *Walker, London,* starring the tiny but lovely Mary Ansell, played to packed houses. James M. Barrie was now a famous playwright as well as a world-renowned novelist.

Soon Mary and Jamie became a couple. Still, it wasn't until he went home to visit his mother in Scotland in 1894, caught pneumonia, nearly died, and Mary left the cast of the play to go north to nurse him, that things turned serious. They were married at his mother's house a few months later and took up residence in London.

"Wendy (aghast), don't you know what a kiss is?"

FROM PETER PAN, THE PLAY

Every day, rain or shine, wearing a greatcoat several sizes too big for him and a bowler hat, Jamie walked his huge Saint Bernard dog, Porthos, in London's Kensington Gardens. The dog liked to stand on its hind feet with its paws on Jamie's shoulders.

While walking in the Gardens, Jamie came upon a curly haired four-year-old named George Llewelyn Davies, out with his younger brother, Jack, and their nanny.

Soon the boys were playing games with Jamie and his dog, the nanny sternly looking on. Jamie could wiggle his ears, do magic, tell wild stories just as he had as a boy in the upstairs room. He could make up plays as he had with Robb in the washhouse. He led the boys in pirate games, just as he had with his childhood friend Stuart in Dumfries Academy. Sometimes he and the boys sailed boats on Round Pond. These games went on for months, Jamie as much a boy as Jack and George.

"I don't want ever to be a man,"
he said with passion.
"I want always to be a little boy and to have fun."

FROM **PETER AND WENDY**

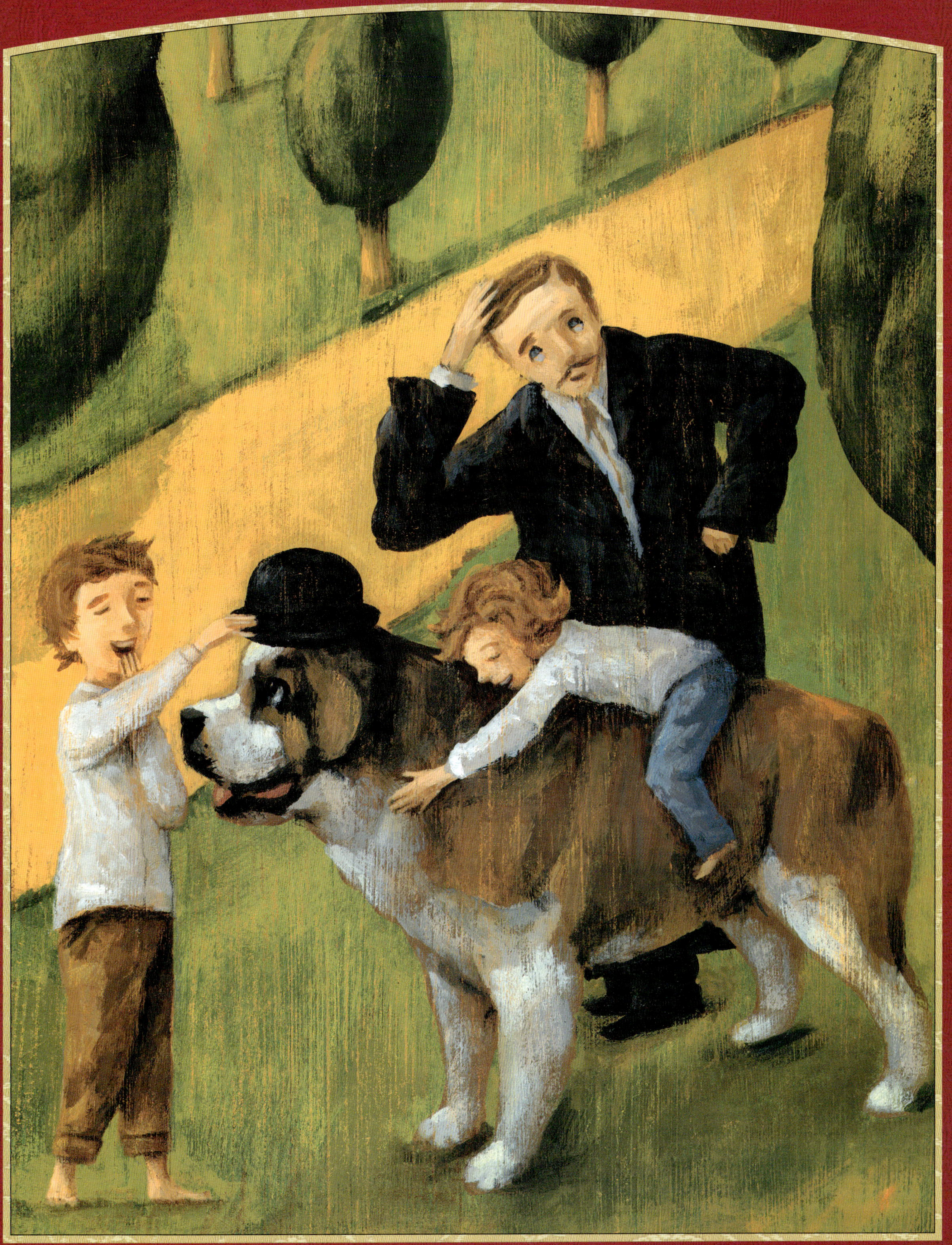

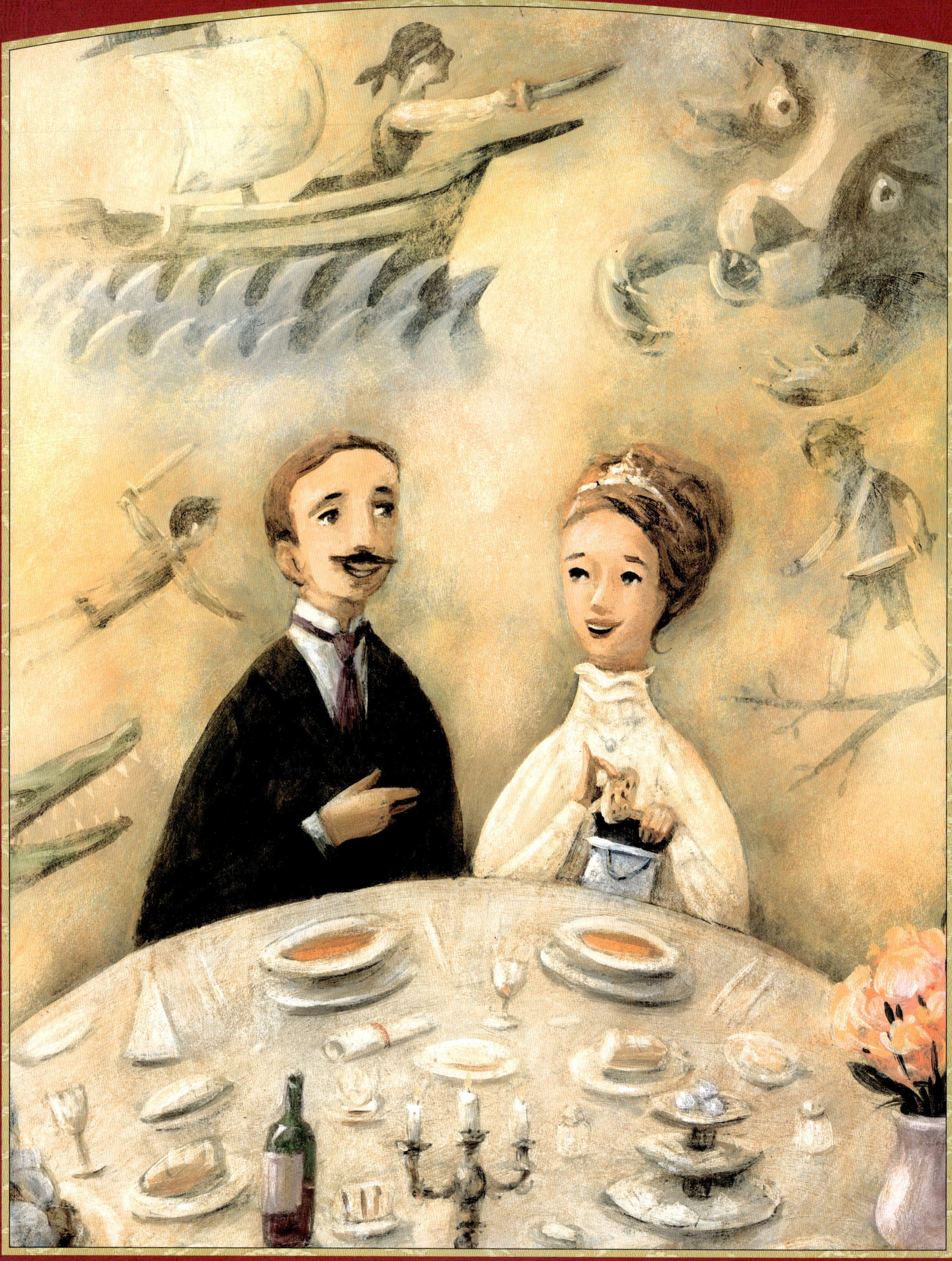

At a New Year's Eve dinner, Jamie sat next to a beautiful woman named Sylvia Llewelyn Davies. He noticed that she was taking sweets from the table and hiding them in her handbag. "For Peter," she told him, not for herself. It turned out that she was George and Jack's mother, and Peter was another of her sons. In all she had four boys, soon to be five.

Jamie introduced himself as the mystery man with the great dog from Kensington Gardens who played with her children. Delighted, Sylvia invited him to visit them at home.

Soon, Jamie and his wife, Mary, were going on holidays with the Llewelyn Davies family, renting cottages at Black Lake within a five-minute walk from one another.

When he was not working on his new plays, Jamie entertained the boys. He created haunted groves, wrecked islands, and black lagoons. An old punt became a pirate ship; Porthos, in a tiger mask, a ferocious beast.

"Sometimes he fell like a spinning-top from sheer merriment."

FROM PETER PAN IN KENSINGTON GARDENS

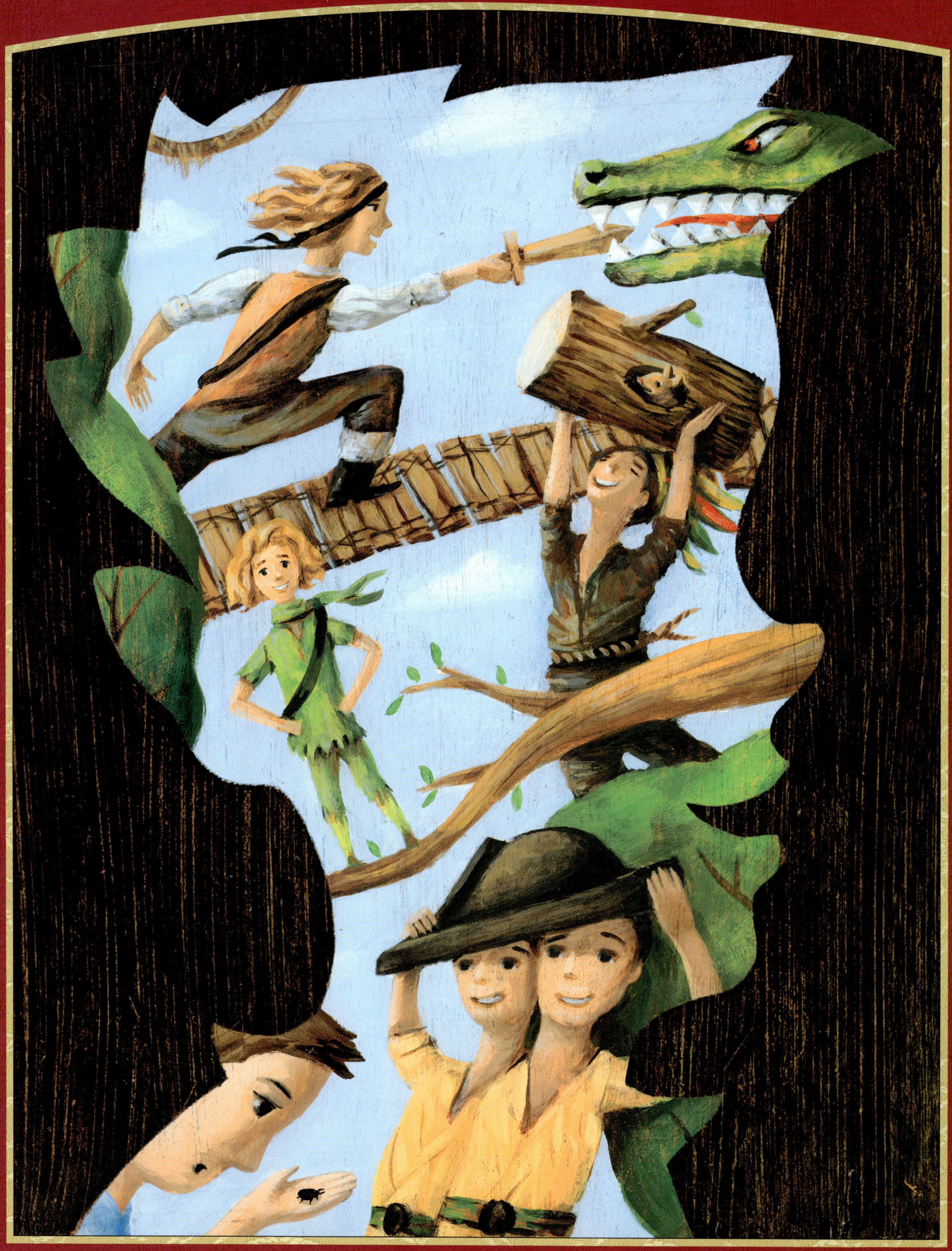

For the next six years, Jamie was a huge part of the Llewelyn Davis family, even while his own marriage was falling apart.

Then in 1904, he began writing the play that would become his masterpiece—*Peter Pan*. It used all of the games that he and the boys loved: pirates, Indians, fairies, as well as beasts like the crocodile. It had a family dog called Nana who looked a great deal like Porthos.

Jamie wrote to the Llewelyn Davies boys that the Peter Pan character was based on them. "I always knew that I made Peter by rubbing the five of you violently together, as savages with two sticks produce a flame."

"Keep back, lady,
no one is going to catch me and make me a man."
FROM PETER AND WENDY

By local theater standards the play was huge. There were over fifty characters, and four of them were supposed to fly. A fairy light had to be made so that it could go about the stage. Jamie was sure the play was too expensive to be produced. He even promised his agent he would give him another play if the first lost money. But the agent loved it from the beginning and insisted the role of Peter be played by an actress, as it has been ever since.

Rehearsals began in October. All the actors were pledged to keep the play a secret. In fact, most of them were only given the scenes in which they had lines. Even the actress playing Peter knew little about the play. On arriving at the theater, she was horrified to learn that she couldn't go onstage until her life had been insured for the flying scenes. But rumors got out, and soon the theater's management had to hire extra guards to keep reporters from sneaking into rehearsals, which went on for six weeks.

However, Sylvia Llewelyn Davies was invited to bring the boys to a rehearsal. Not only were they the reason Jamie had written the play, but Sylvia's brother, a famous actor, had been cast in the double role of Mr. Darling and Captain Hook.

Jamie stopped rehearsals in order to give the boys each a turn in the flying harness.

"Wake up," she cried,
"Peter Pan has come and he is to teach us to fly."
FROM PETER AND WENDY

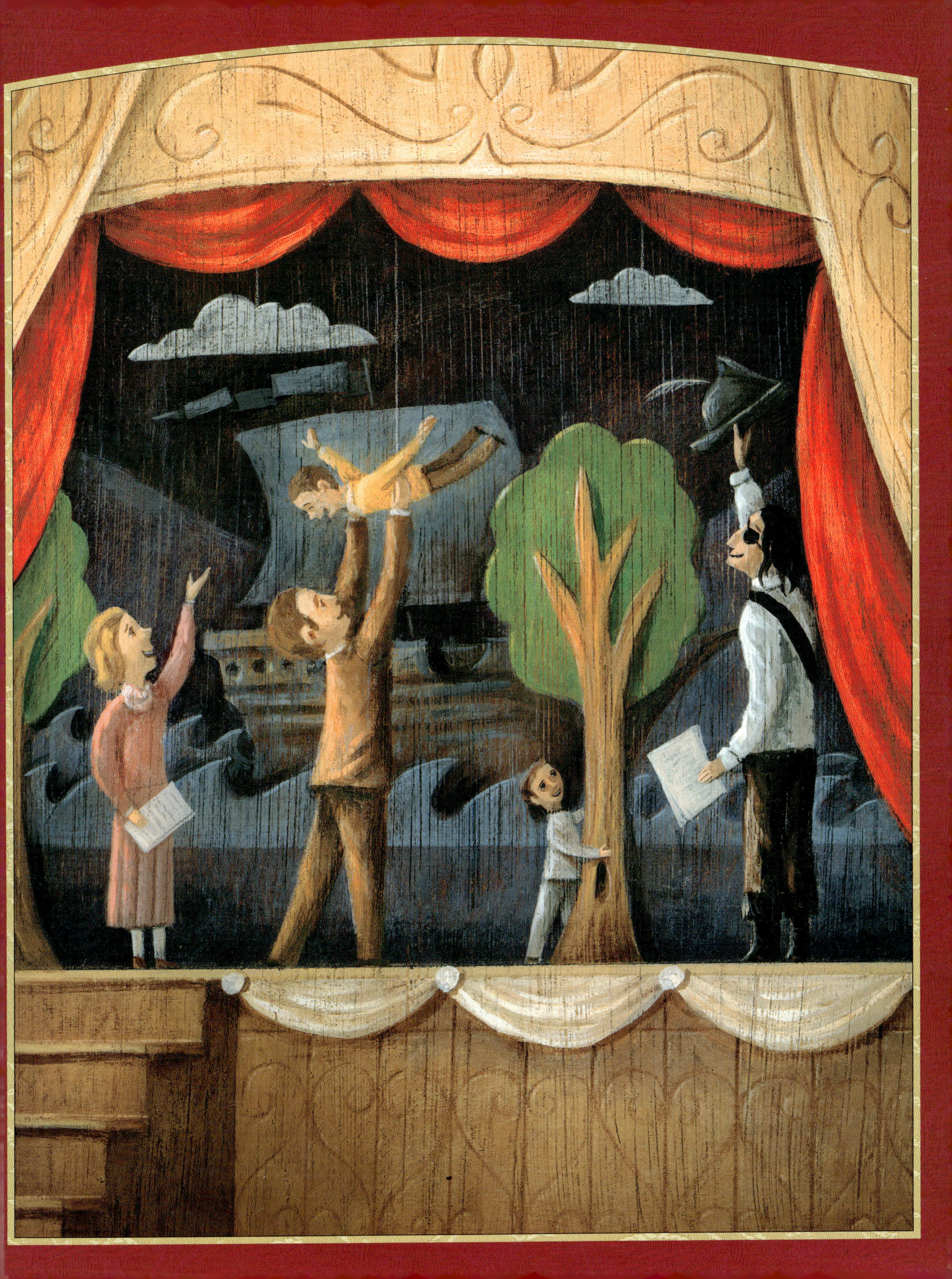

When the curtain went up on opening night, there was a great hush. The audience of mostly adults watched as the dog Nana got the bath ready for a small boy. After that there were hoots of laughter and gasps of delight as the audience was entirely pulled into the fantasy.

Despite Barrie's fears, the opening December 27, 1904, in London, was an immediate success. The actors were brought back again and again for bows. The applause went on and on and on.

A cablegram sent to the agent in New York read: PETER PAN ALRIGHT. LOOKS LIKE A BIG SUCCESS. What an understatement!

By 1928, when the script was published, it had grown from three acts to five.

Asking the audience to clap their hands if they believed in fairies was first done by the actress Maude Adams when she played the role of Peter in the first New York City production.

In 1908, a final scene was added to the play, in which a grown-up Wendy lets her child Jane fly off to Neverland with the still-young Peter to help him with his spring cleaning. It was only used for one performance.

"One of the great differences between the fairies and us is that they never do anything useful."

FROM PETER PAN IN KENSINGTON GARDENS

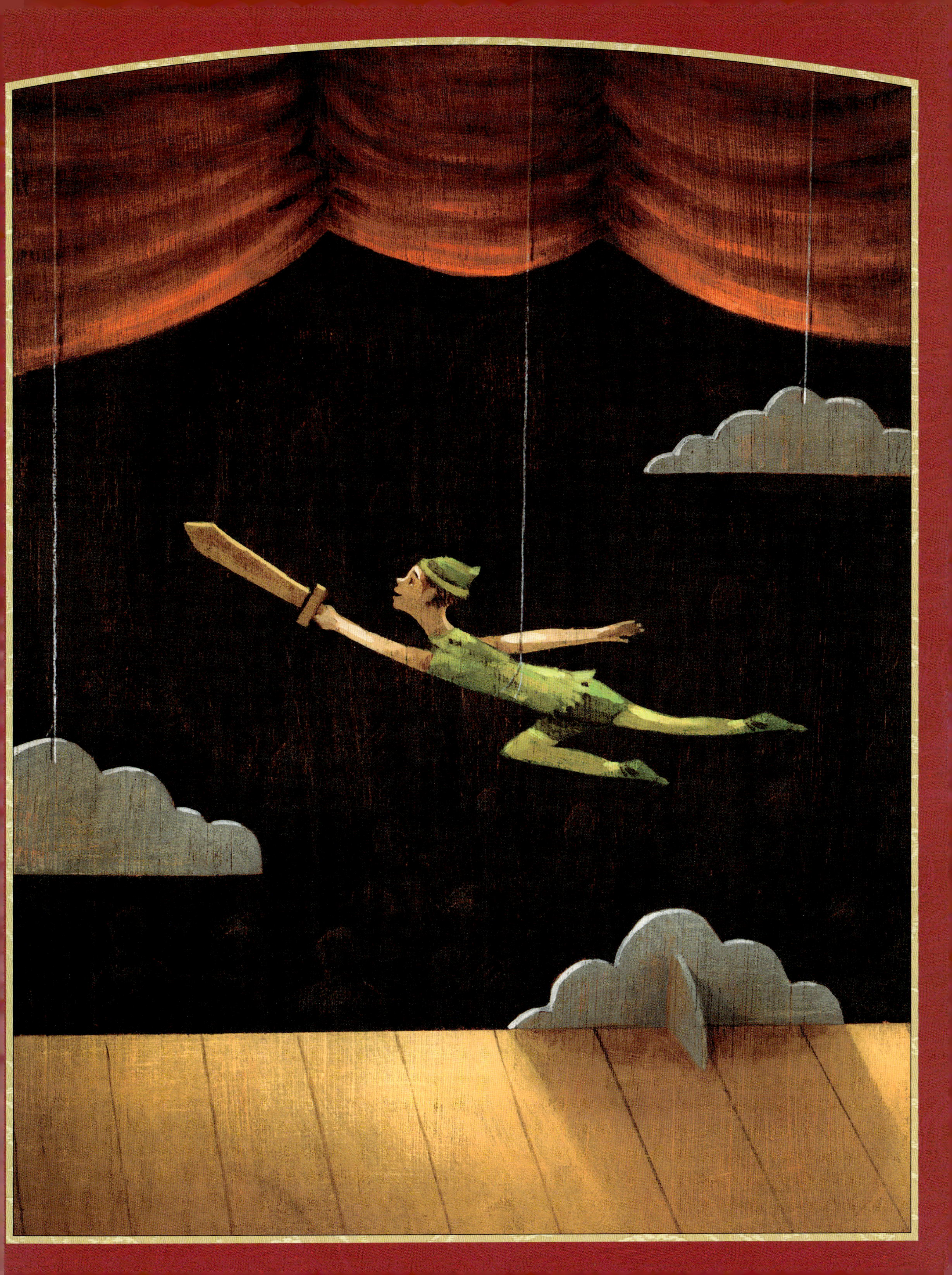

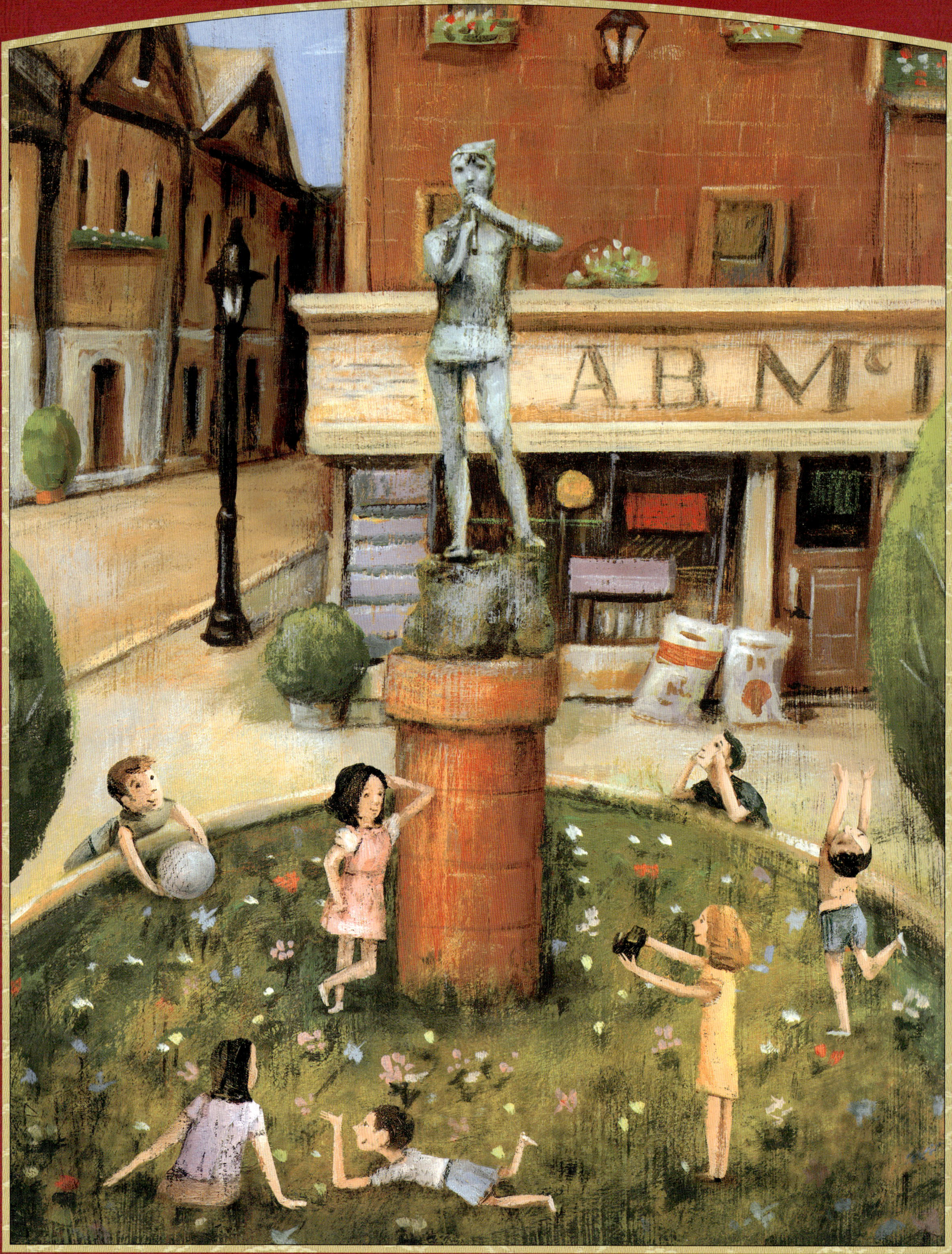
A.B. Mc

Three years after the first performance of *Peter Pan*, the Llewellyn Davies boys' father died of cancer. Jamie often sat by his bedside reading to him. He made a promise that he would help raise the boys.

Sylvia died three years after that, also of cancer. "Uncle Jim"—as the boys called him—became the boys' official guardian. Though the older boys were no longer J. M. Barrie's playmates (George being seventeen, Jack sixteen), they were all good fishing companions, and *his* boys till the end.

When Jamie died thirty years later, in 1937, he had already gifted the copyright for *Peter Pan* to the Great Ormond Hospital for Sick Children in London, which meant that any money made from the book, the play, and associated sales, went to the hospital. At Great Ormond, there is a Peter Pan Ward, a Barrie Wing, a Peter Pan café, a plaque in the chapel, and a bronze statue of Peter Pan. Other Peter Pan statues can be found in Kensington Gardens and in the town of Barrie's birth, Kirriemuir.

Some of Barrie's many plays and books are still read or occasionally performed, but it is *Peter Pan* who truly lives. He lives on in books, in comics, onstage; he lives on in short stories, song lyrics, poems; he lives in video games and pinball games; he lives in the movies as well, both animated and live action. There is a Peter Pan bus company and Peter Pan peanut butter, and hundreds of other items named after him.

Barrie, who never had any children of his own, not only adopted and raised the Llewelyn Davies boys, he helped—and continues to help—hundreds of thousands more children. And though Peter Pan is a make-believe character, everyone knows where he lives.

"Second star to the right and straight on until morning."

FROM PETER PAN, THE PLAY

A selection of works by J. M. Barrie:

BANDELERO, THE BANDIT, 1877 (play)
BETTER DEAD, 1888
THE LITTLE MINISTER, 1891
IBSEN'S GHOST, 1891 (play)
WALKER, LONDON, 1892 (play)
TOMMY AND GRIZEL, 1896
SENTIMENTAL TOMMY: THE STORY OF HIS BOYHOOD, 1896
THE LITTLE WHITE BIRD, 1902 (note: Peter Pan appeared first time)
THE ADMIRABLE CRICHTON, 1902 (play)
PETER PAN OR THE BOY WHO WOULD NOT GROW UP, 1904
PETER PAN IN KENSINGTON GARDENS, 1906
PETER AND WENDY, 1911
DEAR BRUTUS, 1917
THE OLD LADY SHOWS HER MEDALS, 1917 (play)
RECONSTRUCTING THE CRIME, 1917 (play)
DEAR BRUTUS, 1917 (play)
THE BOY DAVID, 1936 (play)

These famous actresses (and many others) have played Peter Pan:

Nina Boucicault—the first Peter
Maude Adams—the first American Peter
Pauline Chase—Barrie's favorite Peter

Jean Forbes-Robertson	Maggie Smith
Hayley Mills	Jean Arthur
Eva Le Gallienne	Sandy Duncan
Mary Martin	Cathy Rigby

"You just think lovely wonderful thoughts and they lift you up in the air."

FROM PETER PAN